# Don't Quit Your Day Job

## 7 Steps to Discover & Launch Your Passion Into Profits While You're Still Employed

## Shyra Smith

ISBN: 0692466401
ISBN 13: 9780692466407

# Why I Wrote This Book

*"If you are willing and obedient, you
shall eat the good of the land."*

*— Isaiah 1:19*

**MY FATHER WAS** a pastor when I was growing up
so I spent a lot of time in church. As a kid, I remember
the Bible talked about how lovely it was in heaven; how
happy and peaceful things were up there. I remember
thinking to myself, "I want to have that now, I don't
want to have to die to have that kind of life!". I wanted
to see this pleasant way of living here on Earth and I
wanted to prove to myself that I could have the peace
and happiness that the Bible described was in Heaven.

I believed in my heart I could have that "Heavenly" life, here and now, and I didn't have to wait to get to heaven to have it.

When I was growing up, I didn't have many role models to look up to. Many of the people around me lived in "the struggle"; they would spend their money on what I call "foolishness" (alcohol, drugs, clubbing, etc..) and then would show up to church on Sunday putting on their "Christian" act. The way they were living didn't add up to me and I knew, even then, that I had to break free from "the struggle" mentality. I wanted more for my life than what I was seeing.

I also knew I was different; that there was a higher calling on my life; however, as a child, I was surrounded by a lot of limiting beliefs. Some were my own, and most were in the people around me. At a very young age, I discovered if I wanted to have a better life for myself, *change* had to start with me. So, I planned my "escape".

It was 1995 and I was 22 years old. I chose to move away from my friends and family because I knew I needed to breakaway from what was familiar to me. I needed to learn how to become the person I was destined to be and I had to do it on my own. I didn't want to continue to "fall back" on family members for help and had to figure out how to survive in the "real" world, and the REAL world was scary.

I packed up my old, beat up car with a suitcase full of clothes and with only three hundred dollars on a credit card, I made my way to Dallas.  Dallas was the unknown, the place that birthed big dreams and I had BIG dreams for my life.  When I got to "the Big City", things didn't go as planned and I found myself having to find a place to lay my head at night. After all, being homeless was definitely NOT part of the BIG dreams I had for myself.  I ended up finding a cheap motel room (a roach motel) and put my trust in God that everything would work out.

I had dug myself into a hole that I was determined to not be in for long.  I knew my faith would be tested but I didn't want to quit and run back home to my Mother.  After all, I was no longer a kid. Within a couple of weeks, my situation began to turn around, in fact, miracles started to happen for me.

I found a job very quickly and on my first day at work, someone introduced me to a person who had a room for rent. At that point, I only had the money left on my credit card and didn't have any money to pay them until my first paycheck. Even though I didn't know the person well, something told me to trust them.  I was honest about my situation and informed them that I wouldn't be able to pay them until payday. The person let me move in and we agreed I would pay them when I received my check in two weeks.

My first "test" came when, after two weeks, my car broke down. I had to make a decision: do I keep my word to my landlord or do I get my car fixed. I didn't have enough money to do both. I made the decision to keep my word and pay my rent and on that very same day, I received a phone call from a co-worker telling me his friend owned a dealership and was willing to help me get a new car.

Initially, I was a bit doubtful, but something came over me that said, "just trust it's going to be okay". A tow truck was sent over and I was blessed with a new (to me) car. It was a cute Honda Accord hatchback that I'd always wanted.

I share this story because, while my decision to keep my word to my landlord may seem like no big deal, what I learned was how important my faith and honoring my word truly is. I chose to do the right thing and in the end, I was rewarded for it. I had a nice place to live *and* I got a brand new car. This awareness helped me turn my whole life around and I began to reap the rewards of my faith in action.

Since 1995, I've been able to create a life many people only dream of; my husband and I own a thriving business, we run a non-profit youth organization and get to do a lot of fun things with my family without having to worry about money. My lifestyle is stress-free, happy and well balanced; far from what it was when I first arrived in Dallas.

I realized I could help a lot of people with what I've learned from my own journey and that's why I've written this book. I want to share the life lessons and steps I took to get where I am today. I believe that if you're equipped in mind and spirit, and do the right things in the right way, you can have a "heavenly" life right now.

I want to reach individuals who are craving change in hopes that I may be able to help create some positive change in their lives. My husband and I have helped many people elevate their lives with our mentoring and in the following pages, I trust you will find inspiration to go out and live your dreams and passions too.

## Why You Should Read This Book

**LAUNCHING A BUSINESS** is a scary endeavor. It involves many unknowns and a lot of risk. For the dreamer in all of us, we wish to be doing something we're passionate about while getting financially rewarded for it. The biggest obstacle for most people is figuring out what they're passionate about and coming up with a plan to monetize it. The second biggest obstacle is leaving the security of a job to take on The Dream.

Six months before getting married, my husband and I launched our first business, which we still operate today. We invested a lot of time researching, reading, and studying successful people and then implementing what we learned. After launching our business, we both worked full-time and worked the business part-time.

We both went through the process that is outlined in this book and combined our strengths and talents to create our primary business.

This book will give you – in a nutshell - a head start; it will guide you step-by-step on what you will need to have in place to launch your business while you're still employed and give you a blueprint to turn your passions into profit.

As a business mentor, I focus on two sides of development: Personal Growth and Business Development/ Growth Strategies.  I believe personal development is a crucial aspect in business because in most cases, it's the limiting belief system that causes people and businesses to fail within the first three years.  So I help my clients bring together their personal development and their business brand to create a strong presence in the marketplace. Your company is a reflection of YOU and you must be willing to grow and adapt in an ever-changing business environment.

The steps I'll be sharing in the following pages help build a foundation for success. That's why I say, "Don't Quit Your Day Job!",... just yet.  This book will help you discover what your passions are, what you want (in life & in business) and why, and how to structure your business around your lifestyle... all while you're still reaping the benefits and security of a job.  It will help you make your transition from an employee to a business owner a little less stressful and a lot more fulfilling.

In the process, you'll become a person of integrity, passion and success.  Thank you for reading!

# Table of Contents

# 1

## Who Is Shyra Smith: The Struggle, The Shift, & The Breakthrough

**BEFORE WE DIVE** into the good stuff, I want to share a little bit more about my story and who I am. First and foremost, I am a woman of profound Faith. My belief in God is my foundation. HE is at the core of my (and my family's) life. I am a Wife and a Mother; a Daughter and Sister; a Granddaughter and an Aunt. I am an entrepreneur and a philanthropist. I'm a marketing guru, speaker and author. I am a Weekday Pamperess and purveyor of fine dining. I'm a chauffeur (to my children) and a mighty fine chef (for family and friends). And most of all, I'm **grateful** for being able to be, do and have all of the things I love and enjoy.

My husband and I own HS3 Enterprises, in which we help business owners find talented staff, implement solid IT strategies and help them grow their bottom line. Our goal is to assist our clients in succeeding in every aspect of their business.

We also run a non-profit organization called Triumph Youth Sports, which was inspired by our children. We focus on cultivating and developing young athletes into leaders on and off the field. Our goal is to assist young athletes develop a positive self-image on a physical, emotional and social level. Among their peers, our participants excel in their chosen sport and in their life because of the fundamental lessons we teach in our program.

We have also designed a social club for our married friends who are in business together. We call this organization Elevating Couples in Business. We organize gatherings to share dinner, cultivate bonding and connectedness and create new memories with one another. One of my passions is bringing people together and trying new things. Being able to give people the opportunity to experience something new for the first time brings me pure joy.

One of my greatest accomplishments in life are my children, Cayden and Jaren. Cayden is a quick-witted, laid back and kindhearted kid who thrives on the football and baseball field. Jaren is an artist and lives for soccer and track. I'm proud to be called their Mom because they are both leaders in their lives. One of my proudest moments as a parent came when Cayden changed his school policies because of a bullying incident he went through and he did it all on his own.

My family and I live a happy and stress-free life now, but it wasn't always like this. We faced many challenges and struggles along the way and we don't take anything for granted.

IT ALL CAME CRASHING DOWN

It was the early 2000s. My husband and I were newly-weds - happy and full of blissful matrimony — we had just begun our new life together as we settled into our newly built home and had begun operating our newly established business in information technology.

I was pregnant with our first son, Cayden. My husband had taken on our business full-time and I kept my full-time job and helped work our business part-time. Life was looking good. We were on the road to success.

Then we woke up to the worst days of our lives. The Dotcom bubble had burst and was taking our business with it. Day after day, the stock market news didn't look good for the IT arena. We were clutched with fear about what was going to happen since the IT market crashed. Then the *whole market* crashed. And we were paralyzed. We didn't know what to do next. We were about to lose everything we'd worked so hard for.

It was a scary time for a lot of people, including us. I watched my husband's peace of mind deteriorate day after day and there were times I felt helpless, but we stood by each other and spoke kind words of encouragement to one another. After the shock of the stock market crash had settled, we received notice that we were about to lose our home.

It seemed like we were on a fast downward spiral and we were scared. We were stuck in our fear once again.

Once we came to our senses and after a lot of prayer, we began doing what was necessary to get ourselves out of this hole. My husband had to swallow his pride and began looking for work because my income alone wasn't cutting it. Most employers turned him away for being "over-qualified", but he eventually found a part-time job in construction to help with our bills. This was the lowest point in our lives as a couple.

During this time, we had a heart-to-heart talk about our situation and agreed we never wanted to be in this situation again. We also knew we didn't want to give up on our dreams; we'd made a commitment to each other that we would do whatever it took to actualize our dreams - we were in this together.

We recognized this was our "test" and we had to muster up the courage and strength to pull ourselves out of this situation. We knew we had God by our side. We began brainstorming and came up with ideas that we could try in an attempt to save our business. We both now worked full-time and worked the business part-time to not give up on our business. Some of the ideas we came up with got us excited about our business again and we found one idea we thought we could run with.

After some lengthy research, we knew we had a huge opportunity in our hands. We realized, even with the state of the economy, there were still businesses out there that needed our services and there were A LOT of businesses still willing to pay for our services. The only problem was, we were a two-person team.

This was another "test". At this point, we'd put so much energy and effort into rebooting our business there was no way we could stop. There was too much momentum.

We decided this was our moment to rise above our challenges and become the people we were meant to be. So, we took another chance on ourselves and went "all in". We began reaching out to independent contractors and brought them in as we brought in clients. We did everything we were guided to do and worked hard to turn our situation around. It wasn't easy for us, but it worked and it saved not only our home and business, but our lives.

### The Climb Back Up

It took us many months to build up our clientele, but after a while, we discovered our niche and began attracting more and more business. The obstacles we faced during that time tested our faith, our bond and our commitment. We both look back on that time and laugh at ourselves because of the ways we acted towards one another. I couldn't have asked for a better partner to go through something like that with. I watched my husband transform right before my eyes and become the man he (and I) always knew he was; a man of faith, courage and integrity. And I realized what can happen when two people come together and work through challenges in a positive and supportive manner. Don't get me wrong, there were times when we weren't so nice to one another, but in the thick of it, we kept our commitment and our promise to each other.

We have a lot to be grateful for in our lives now. We worked hard to regain our piece of heaven here on Earth, even though we had to go through hell to get here.

We believed in our dream, we believed in each other and we believed we could have it all. We're living proof this kind of life is possible. There's just a lot of work to get there.

And if you're willing to do the work, you'll be rewarded with the life you desire. There's no easy road to success but there are many road signs along the way to help you get there and these are just a few of them.

I started this book with my all time favorite passage from the Bible and I will end this chapter with it too:

> *"If you are willing and obedient, you will eat the good of the land."*
>
> — ISAIAH *1:19*

Our time here on Earth is limited so we should enjoy it as best as we can.  When you put forth the work that is required rather than putting forth excuses, you can obtain the lifestyle you truly desire.  We wish you all the best life has to offer.

# 2

## Step 1: Find a Mentor – Why Having One (Or Not Having One) Could Make or Break Your Business

**STARTING A BUSINESS** from scratch is like jumping into the deep end of the pool when you don't know how to swim. This is, essentially, what most people do when they're first starting out as a new business owner. All too often, this is what leads to drowning and contributes to the "failure in less than three years" statistic. We are all about taking the leap, but not in blind faith. We take the leap in what we like to call, prepared faith.

When you have a family to support, starting a business in blind faith could lead to health problems, marital problems, financial problems and (as statistics show) a failed business. When you have a failed business, this impacts your inner life as well; depression occurs, you begin to feel "less than" as a human being and most likely, you have to start all over. You go back to the workforce and now you have to face the humiliation of "trying and failing". The worst thing you can hear, is that old saying, "hey, at least you tried". This is the harsh reality most unprepared entrepreneurs face.

We believe that in order to *go for the gold* in business, it is best to find someone who can mentor you. It's like having a swim coach if you want to go to the Olympics. A business mentor can see all the things you don't see because they have the experience, the expertise and know how. They've made all of the mistakes and know what to do when you run into an obstacle. They see the obstacle far before you do and can point them out before you come up against them. They want you to succeed and will push you, encourage you and cheer you on. They're your number one fan.

WHAT TO LOOK FOR IN A BUSINESS MENTOR
Not all business mentors are created equal. Find one you connect with. I recommend honing in on these key areas during your search.

1. **Lifestyle:**
   Are they living the way you want to live? Do they have the things you want to have? Are they walking their talk? There has been a surge in the coaching industry lately and many people think that because they have gone through a Coaching Certification Course, it gives them a

license to tell people what to do in their lives. Be wary of these people.  Not all certified coaches are equipped to handle another person's problems. Make sure to do your research and go through an interview process. The main thing to ask about is their RESULTS. What kind of results do they have in their lives? And this doesn't mean just financial results; while this is a very important aspect, you want to get a clear view of the whole picture. Don't be afraid to ask them about their results in the areas that are important to YOU.  The best analogy I can give is this: you would never ask a broke person how to get rich, nor would you ever ask an overweight person how to lose weight. They will give you some advice, but would you ever listen to them? So, when looking for a mentor, ask yourself if their lifestyle matches the lifestyle you desire. If the answer is yes, move forward. If the answer is no, it's okay to tell them they're not the right fit.

2. **Length of Time In Business:**
   What's the difference between a novice and a professional? TIME and PRACTICE. Think about something you're really great at, something you truly excel at that you could do with your eyes closed. How did you become excellent at it? Practice, right? And practice takes time. My children excel in their chosen sport because

they rarely ever miss practice. It's the same when looking for someone to mentor you; the longer they've been in business means the more successful knowledge and experience they will have to share with you. If they're any good, they'll have been in business for five years or more. You want to work with the pros because you're in the game to get the life you desire. You're in the game to win and if they're winning, chances are they'll be able to guide you in the right direction.

3. **Core Values Alignment:**
   You want to find someone whose core values align with yours.  If one of your core values is Faith and your potential mentor or coach is a non-believer, you're going to run into some problems. You want someone who understands you on a CORE level because they will "get you" and you will "get them".  There's an unspoken understanding you'll share with one another and that kind of connection is priceless.

4. **Integrity:**
   This ties into "lifestyle" in the saying, "do they walk their talk".  This statement says a lot about integrity.  We all know that person who wears the most up to date fashions, yet can't pay their light bill; or drives an overly expensive car and is borrowing money to pay their rent. There's a big

disconnect there and you want to find a mentor who **honors their WORD**. For example, if you agree on an appointment time for Wednesday at 10:30AM, and they don't communicate with you if they're going to be late or miss the call completely with no explanation, this is a lack of integrity. Integrity means showing up when you're supposed to and being in communication if you're unable to meet the committed time or agreement. And here's the rub, YOU are bound to this agreement too, so integrity is a two way street. So, this means if they haven't shown up, they may be waiting on you! Always be clear on your scheduled appointments and agree on who should be calling whom.

You may be wondering how those two previous examples tie into integrity. *Integrity is also a matter of priorities*. Read that again. When you move into a home, you enter to an agreement with the light company and the *agreement* is they will provide you with a service and you agree to pay them within a specified timeframe; same with the rent scenario. What good will it do if you can't see yourself in the mirror when you're putting on your fancy clothes or you're living out of your expensive car if you can't pay your rent or you don't have a successful business because you didn't show up to your scheduled session?

Now, that's not to say that life doesn't get in the way, but integrity is about *honoring your agreement*. If you can't pay your light bill or rent on time, do you call the light company or landlord to let them know when you can pay or do you let them chase after you? When you obtain a mentor who operates with integrity, it's a guarantee that they will show up for you. That's their commitment to YOU, and if they are unable to make their committed time, they will be in communication to schedule a new time. If they aren't, this is a big red flag; however, you must be willing to reach out too. If they don't respond, this should not be taken lightly. Your livelihood is on the line and a mentor with integrity will be just as committed, if not more, to your success than you are. Remember, agreements are also collaborations; your success is dependent upon whether you show up to play. Your mentor will show up because they have partnered with you and care about your success.

5. **Transparency:**
   A great business mentor will tell you the truth, no matter what.

   Let's say your dream is to open a restaurant. You tell them this and they hesitate, then go on to tell you this is something they are well versed in. You caught on to their hesitation, but you decide to move forward anyway. Three months into your contract, you notice they've missed important meetings, haven't been in communication and for some strange reason, have fallen off the face of the earth. They're nowhere to be found. After numerous phone calls and emails, they finally get back to you and come clean. They had no idea what they were doing and in good faith, they offer you a refund. At this point, you're in a time deficit, financial deficit and emotional deficit because you were stuck figuring things out on your own.  A great business mentor would NEVER do this to you.

If they know they cannot help you, for any reason, they will tell you honestly. They know time is a commodity and they will not waste your time or theirs.

WHAT MENTORS ARE LOOKING FOR IN YOU

When you enter into an agreement with a business mentor it becomes a collaborative effort. Their job is to show up for you and your job is to show up for yourself. They already know what's possible for your life because they have been where you are and know what it's like on the other side.  They believe in you before you believe in yourself.

This is what a great mentor will expect of you:

1. **An unwavering commitment to your goals:**
   Your personal business mentor already knows you can have the life you desire even when you don't yet think it's possible. They know you can have it all. There will be moments you will want to throw in the towel and give up on your goals and they will support your choice no matter what, but you *must* commit yourself to following through as if your life depended on it, because it does. They will be there to guide you and encourage you when the going gets rough, but it's up to you to muster up the strength to carry on. They know this is a marathon not a sprint, and are just as committed to your dreams as you are.

2. **Integrity.**
   See the section above. This is a two way street and you must show up when you say you're going to and honor your agreements no matter how small. This also ties into your commitment to your goals.

3. **Drive:**
   They can't and won't do everything for you. You must be self-motivated to accomplish your goals and take the wheel while they help you navigate the streets to launching your business successfully. Think of them as your navigator on the road trip to launching your business. They

will give you all the tools you need to succeed but you have to do the driving.

4. **A willingness to be mentored:**
   Your mentor knows things you don't know, which means that they will be asking you to do things you've never done. This can and will get uncomfortable, but this is where great things happen. When you're open and willing to take on the mentoring that's being provided, you will begin to see results. What you resist persists, so be willing to take the mentoring that is being given to you.

5. **A willingness to grow:**
   Personal development is important to all great mentors because they know the biggest breakthroughs happen when there is a shift in mindset. You must approach this endeavor with a beginner's mind and be willing to grow into this experience with your mentor's assistance. They will help you see things about yourself you never saw before and sometimes it can feel confrontational, but when you follow through, you'll become the person you always knew yourself to be.

Having a great business mentor by your side as you start your journey as an entrepreneur puts you at a greater advantage for success. You'll be able to leverage their expertise, resources and network to accomplish your goals and live the life you are meant to live.

# 3

## Step 2: Know What You Want & Why You Want It In All Areas Of Your Life

"**WHAT DO YOU** want?" This question stops a lot of people in their tracks. Most people have a hard time deciding what they want for dinner let alone what they want in their life and business. How many times have you set your New Years resolutions only to end up right back where you started? We all have been there but in order to get the life you desire, you must have clear goals and know why you want to achieve them. It's not enough to set the goal, there has to be fuel to propel you towards them and knowing why will get you connected on a deeper level to your goals.

It's important to have goals and have them written down. There's something that happens when you take pen to paper and write down your goals. It crystallizes them into your memory and you're more likely to accomplish them if you have them written.

When my husband and I got married, we both sat down and listed everything we wanted as a couple, as individuals and as a family. Launching our business was one of those things.  We included things we didn't get to experience when we were growing and as our business began to flourish, we were able to check those things off one by one. We continually add new goals and experiences to our list and every year, our goals get bigger and bigger.

List Your Wants & Goals To Achieve Them
Since you're still employed, I'm going to assume you have a limited number of hours you'll be able to dedicate to your business; however, this is a foundational piece to launching your business.  I encourage you to make time for this, even if it's only half an hour a day (on your lunch break) so you can get very clear on the things that are important to you.  Without this piece, you'll be building your business on quicksand and we want to build it on a solid foundation. If you're married or have a family, this is a great exercise to do with your partner and your children.

This exercise will walk you through step-by-step on how to create a S.M.A.R.T goal.  This stands for:

**S**pecific – Be specific about what you want.
Imagine you want a new car, you go into the dealership and you say to the salesman, "I want a new car".

The first thing he'll ask you is, "what kind of new car do you want?", and you say, "I don't know, I just want a new car." Well, he'll give you a blank stare and may ask you to leave and come back when you know what you want. Unfortunately, this is the way most people approach goal setting.  People who have vague goals get vague results or no results! So be specific about what you want.  Now, if you were to walk into a dealership and tell the salesman you want a 2015 Honda Accord EX with tan leather seats, a Bose stereo system, anti-lock breaks, sunroof, GPS system and XM Radio, you'll have a better chance of getting exactly what you want. You'll avoid many a blank stares when you're specific about what you want.

Measurable – Your goal must be measurable.
Crafting a goal is like cooking from a recipe. Let's say we're baking a chocolate cake; for this cake we'll need *specific* ingredients (flour, milk, eggs, chocolate, etc.) and those ingredients will need to be measured out: 2 cups of flour, 1 cup of milk, 2 eggs and 1 ½ cups of cocoa powder.  When you're crafting your goal, how is your result measured? If your goal were to lose weight, how many pounds would you like to lose? If your goal is to write a 200-page book, how many pages do you need to write everyday? If your goal is to make $10k a month, how many clients do you need? If your goal is measured it will lend itself to being a clear and concise goal.

**A**ctionable – What steps must you take in order to move your goal into reality?

Lets go back to the cake example. After you've measured out your ingredients, the next steps are: pre-heat the oven, mix the ingredients in a large bowl, pour the mixture into a bake pan and put the pan in the oven. Having a plan of action is where the rubber meets the road and when you take the steps, it will get you to your goal.

**R**ealistic – We're all big dreamers and want to be instant millionaires when we first launch our business.

I hear this all of the time from my clients, but how realistic is it to make a million dollars in 30, 60 or even 90 days of launching a new business with your current level of knowledge and resources? You must have realistic expectations in your goals and must be wiling to be real and honest with yourself.  It's okay to start small and work your way up to bigger accomplishments. That's how many self-made millionaires have done it.

**T**imely – Within what timeframe are you committing to accomplish your goal?

When you place a deadline on your goal, it creates a structure for you to accomplish it.  When you know something has to be completed by a certain date, you tend to give it more priority. Loosely defined goals without a timeline usually get pushed to the back burner.

Now that we've covered S.M.A.R.T goals, let's look at a few examples of what a clearly defined S.M.A.R.T goal looks like.  First I will list a vague goal, then its S.M.A.R.T counterpart.

*My goal is to lose weight.*
*My goal is to lose 25 lbs by June 1st.*
*My goal is to increase my monthly sales.*
*My goal is to sign 3 additional new clients a month at $3k a piece for the next 12 months.*
*My goal is to write a book.*
*My goal is to write 3 pages a day for the next 100 days.*
*My goal is to learn how to play guitar.*
*My goal is to practice 30 minutes per day and learn one song a week for the next 8 weeks.*
*My goal is to launch a super successful business.*
*My goal is to write a business plan, incorporate my business, research and apply for a small business loan by July 31st.*

Can you see the difference in those examples? Having clearly defined goals will help you turn your big dreams into reality.  Be sure to write down all of the goals you have for every area of your life and don't limit yourself. What would you like to accomplish in the next 5-10 years? Have fun with this and let your imagination run wild!

WHY ARE THESE GOALS IMPORTANT TO YOU?

Now that you've got your goals written down we want to get to the heart of your goals. We want to uncover the emotional drive underneath your wants and discover the spark that lights you up so when you speak about it, people around you get inspired because YOU are inspired by it.

This will be the real reason you jump out of bed every morning and want to do everything you can to make your dreams a reality. Getting to your why is like planning a surprise party for your favorite person on the planet. The goal is to pull the party off without their knowing and the why is to see their reaction. There's a feeling you get when you've pulled it off. See how happy and special they feel *because of you*? What we're after is the feeling you get inside when you see their eyes light up. This is called the burning desire.

So now, the question is, how do you get to your Why? Below are a few examples of goals and whys, so you can get a sense of what I mean.

Goal: Lose 25 lbs by June 1.

Why: So I can fit into that two-piece bikini and feel sexier than ever. (Obviously, this is a man's goal... just kidding!)

Goal: Sign up 3 clients who each pay $3k in the next 90 days.

Why: So I can surprise my daughter with a brand new car on her 16th birthday.

Goal: Read 5 pages a day of *Think and Grow Rich* for the next 30 days.

Why: When I read books like this I increase my value to the market place; more value equals more money, more money means more freedom, freedom means I finally fired my boss!

Goal: To replace my J.O.B income of $_____ within one year of launching my business so I can quit my job and spend every single day with my children.

Why: So I can look my children in the eyes and tell them they can be, do and have anything they want, and mean it. And they'll believe me because I did it.

Goal: To take my wife/husband on the honeymoon we REALLY wanted to take to Tahiti in the next 6 months.

Why: So we can sink our feet in the hot sand, enjoy an ice-cold margarita in peace and quiet... *WITHOUT THE KIDS!*

Goal: To write 3 pages a day of my Self-Help book for the next 100 days.

Why: So I can get my message out to the world and make a difference in somebody's life.

When you are deeply connected to your why, your goals become more attainable. It's a good idea to read your goals and connect with your why on a daily basis. Keep them posted in a place where you can see them every day.

Another way to magnify your goals is to visualize the end result. If you want to lose 25 lbs, imagine yourself in that two-piece bikini soaking in the sun on the white sand beaches of Hawaii. Get connected to the feeling it creates within you, the feeling of having accomplished your goal. This will cultivate the burning desire and fan the flame inside.

The most important part of the S.M.A.R.T goal is the "**A**ctionable" part of your goal. Create a game plan to put into play. In the weight loss example, you might want to hire a personal trainer, schedule out your sessions, come up with a healthy meal plan, go through your pantry and throw away all of the junk food, etc. Once you come up with your plan, commit to following through until you reach your goal. You can start with baby steps, but once you're in practice of being in action, you'll start to see the results you desire in your life.

Creating and accomplishing your goals can be a fun and exciting experience if you let it. You can also get the whole family involved. Goal setting is a great bonding exercise and experience if you have children. This will set them up to be successful adults and give them an advantage in life.

The most successful people in the world set goals, know why they want them and put their plan into action. The operative word here being *ACTION*. Remember, without action, goals are just wishes on paper.

# 4

## Step 3: Take Stock Of Your Natural Talents & Gifts And Cultivate Your Passion!

**THINK BACK TO** your childhood and recall all of the things that brought you pure joy; the things that would make time disappear. One of my fondest memories from my childhood was watching my grandmother cook. I would sit on the kitchen island and watch her in awe as she whipped things up. She made it look so easy and fun and the food always tasted delicious. I also loved watching cooking shows as a child and two of my favorite chefs to watch were Martin Yan and Justin Wilson (he always wore red suspenders and shook his belly when he was mixing ingredients – this would make me laugh every time!). These two guys made cooking fun and entertaining and because of these three influences, I found my passion in cooking. Today, I throw dinner parties for my friends and family and love getting creative in the kitchen.

What were you good at as a kid? Did you tinker with clocks and take things apart then put them back together? Did you like to draw? Did you write poetry or short stories with your friends? Tap into all of the things you enjoyed doing as a child and reconnect with the feeling it brings up. If you could do these things now, would it bring you as much joy? If you haven't done it in a while, let yourself do it. Give yourself this gift so you can reconnect with your joy and passion. Get in the habit of connecting with the feeling of joy in your life. When you cultivate this feeling, other areas of your life will begin to flourish too.

### Name Your Talents & Gifts

Now think of all of the things you're good at now, as an adult. Make a list of all your talents & gifts. Were you gifted with good humor and the ability to write well? Or are you great at giving presentations and sales? Are you good at teaching very complex ideas in a simple way? Are you insanely talented at knitting or have a green thumb? Do you have a particular expertise in something? Write everything down. When you can take stock of what you're naturally good at, it not only boosts your self-confidence, it will give you a starting point for launching your business as well.

If you can connect your talents to your joy, then you'll be on to something. When my husband and I launched HS3 Enterprises, we focused on his talent in the IT arena and I focused on my talent in marketing. We were able to create a viable and thriving business from combining our talents and gifts. This is also a great exercise to do with your partner. If you're stuck, you can ask your partner or friends what they think you're good at.

If you're having a hard time naming your talents and gifts, become "hyperaware" of your day-to-day life and carry a notebook to jot these things down when they become apparent to you. Think about your hobbies, interests and the things you spend your money on. Another way to jog your memory is to list all of the awards and recognition you've received throughout your life.

Once you've compiled your list and have taken stock of what your talents and gifts are, you'll begin to see a pattern emerge.

It's time to take ownership of your natural talents and gifts so you can bring your best offerings to the world!

"GET PAID DOING WHAT YOU LOVE"

Now that you've taken stock of your talents and gifts and have pinpointed one or two things you absolutely love to do, it's time to think about the beliefs that have been holding you back from pursuing your dream. When you read the words, *get paid doing what you love*, what comes up for you? Do you get excited or do you have some self-doubts? Do you believe this can be true for you?

I believe everyone has God given talents and it is also our God given right to bring those talents and gifts to the world.  I also believe you can be handsomely rewarded for it.  Life is truly about doing work we love and are passionate about.  It will take courage and faith to take this leap and once you do, the person you become in the process will astound you. *It IS possible for you!*

Now that you've reconnected with your passions, talents and gifts, it's time to get to work on a few more core pieces before you launch.

# 5

## Step 4: Get Your Life Back In Working Order – Why Restoring Integrity In Your Life Is Important For Your Business

**WHAT DOES IT** mean to restore integrity? First, let's define what integrity truly means. Integrity comes from the root word *integral,* which means, "necessary for completeness; essential or made up of parts forming a whole". *Integrity* means, "completeness, unimpaired condition; soundness and honesty; sincerity".

When you're building a house, you'll need integral parts for the house to be sound and complete. You'll need the foundation, the frame, the electrical & plumbing systems and the walls to have a nice house that you can safely live in. Now imagine a house that's been built without the proper framing and without any load bearing walls. Would you want to live in that house?

So in the "house" that is your life, there are parts of your life that make it whole and complete and allow it to work peacefully and harmoniously. Things like your relationships (wife/husband, kids, parents, friends, etc.), finances, career, hobbies, faith and your mental and physical state. You are at the center of your life; you are the foundation that holds all of these things together. If any of these things are causing you stress, anxiety or making you unhappy, there's something missing that needs to be addressed.

This exercise will require you to be completely honest with yourself about what's working and not working in your life. It will also require you to take 100% responsibility for why things are not working and for finding a resolution. This is where the transformational work begins.

### Determine What's Working In Your Life

Imagine that your life is like a car, it can be any car of your choosing, but it has to be a used car. You know this car could use some work to get it working like new, but since you can't trade in your life, you have to "fix" the things that are not working in order to restore it to "like new" condition. Once you fix these things, you can upgrade to a newer model; the goal is to restore your life back to factory settings, which means back to a healthy and well-oiled, properly running machine. Lets say the engine represents your spirituality/faith, each one of the four tires represents: Relationships (family, friends, spouse, etc.) Finances (career or job), Physical Well-Being, Mental Well-Being (personal development, emotions, etc.), the gas tank represents your passion and desire, and the steering wheel represents you and your ability to steer the car.

Let's imagine all of these parts are in perfect working order; the engine is well oiled, all four tires are full of air you've got a full tank of gas and you're at the top of your game. You are going in to the office and everything is working perfectly. You start the car, punch in the destination on your GPS and you're off; you don't have a care in the world because your car is operating at full integrity and you know you'll arrive at your destination centered and full of confidence ready to rock your presentation at work.

Now, let's imagine that you're getting ready to go on this same trip, but you haven't attended to your spirituality, your husband/wife/child(ren) are upset at you because you haven't come through on that promise for a family vacation in over a year, your boss is on your butt because you missed the last important deadline on a project you're spearheading and you're on the verge of being fired, you've got less than $500 to last you through until your next payday and your credit cards are maxed out, you haven't been eating well and you're so stressed, your hair is falling out! So you get into your car, knowing that the oil is low and you've got four nearly flat tires; the check engine light comes on as soon as you turn the key, you don't even acknowledge your tires are low on air and your gas tank is hovering right above "Empty". You think to yourself, "I've got 30 miles before I need to get gas, I can make it to the office". You put car into gear and head onto the highway. You hit major traffic, and right at that moment, your spouse calls to conveniently remind you of something you forgot to do... again. You lose your temper and have a complete melt down. "POP!" goes your front right tire; you pull over and fall to your knees begging God for a break.

This is an exaggerated example, but for some, it may not be that far from the truth. For some, you might have a strong foundation in your faith, but are up to your eye balls in debt; or you're completely debt free but you're not at your ideal weight and you feel stuck in your career; or you've got a rockin' body, but your relationship with your spouse is on the rocks.

So pinpoint the things in your life that ARE working and write them down. Be completely honest with yourself and don't censor or judge yourself throughout this process. Give yourself a pat on the back for the things that are working, it means you've given these areas priority and attention.

In these areas, which area needs the least attention?

Relationships (Parents, Spouse, Children, Friends, Co-Workers, God, Pets, etc.)

Finances (Income vs. Debt, Bills, etc.)

Physical Well-Being (Exercise, Are You Happy w/ Your Body, etc.)

Mental Well-Being (Emotional, Personal Development, Higher Learning, etc.)

Spirituality/Faith (Are you meditating/praying, reading spiritual texts/inspirational works, etc.)

Hobbies (Are you cultivating your passions?)

Once you've listed what's working, it's time to look at what's not working in your life.

### DETERMINE WHAT'S NOT WORKING IN YOUR LIFE

What ever is left from your list above is a clear indicator of the things you need to work on to get your life back in working order. Take one small step in each of these things to make things right. If your marriage is on the rocks, sit down and have a heart to heart conversation with your spouse and commit to making things right; if you're swimming in debt, take inventory of what you owe and make a commitment to pay it all off; if you're feeling spiritually depleted or disconnected, take time to read an inspirational piece or go to a place of worship; if you're not at your ideal weight, throw out all the sugar and junk food in your house and commit to a workout schedule; if you've been holding on to a grudge with a family member, call them and make amends.

Cleaning up the messes in your life takes a lot of self-honesty and courage. When you take ownership of the things that aren't working and begin to make them right, you'll feel more in control of your destiny and feel more confident about the direction of your life. If you can get your life back to a state of wholeness and integrity, you'll be able to move forward with purpose and passion; and you'll be leading by example. It will open up new avenues for you to show up powerfully for yourself and the people in your life in ways you never thought possible.

### Why This Is Important For Business

We all know that our personal lives can spill into our work life and if things aren't working well at home, it impacts every other aspect of our lives. When your personal life is running like a well-oiled machine, it will give you the confidence you need to start a new endeavor. Your family will be supportive of your dreams, you'll be able to leverage your finances and you'll be empowered and equipped to handle any obstacle that comes your way. While you don't have to wait until everything is "perfect", the mere act of you getting things back in order puts you in the driver's seat of your life. This will build momentum and propel you toward all of the things that are important to you. Most of all, it will give you insight to your own inner game and when you've mastered your inner game, your outer game will begin to line up. Your business is a reflection of you; the more integrity you have in your life, the better off your business will be because you'll be operating from a place of wholeness and stability.

# 6

## Step 5: Gather Your Resources & Begin Building The Structure For Your Business

**BEFORE MY HUSBAND** and I launched our business, we spent months researching and gathering our resources. We read as many books as we could get our hands on and made a list of all of the things that we needed to do in order to get our business up and running. We crunched numbers, got a budget together, sourced the equipment we were going to need, we set up our office and developed our web presence. We also drafted up our contracts, registered the business and opened a bank account.

These are examples of some "behind the scene" things we did before launching our business, but each business may differ according to the industry.

GATHER YOUR RESOURCES

This is where things get very practical and detail ori-
ented. Once you determine what kind of business you
want to launch, it's time to roll up your sleeves, do
some research and get all of your ducks in a row.

**Personal Development**: Get inspired! Stepping
into a new business venture has more to do with your
inner game and a shift in perspective more than anything else. Shifting out of the "employee" mindset
and into a "business owner" mindset is key. In Robert
Kiyosaki's book, *Rich Dad, Poor Dad,* he explains the
differences between being an Employee, being Self-
Employed, being a Business Owner and being an
Investor. These differences are what he calls, The
Cash Flow Quadrant; in other words, how income is
generated in these different business models. As an
"Employee" you work for somebody else and trade
your time for money; when you're "Self-Employed"
you work for yourself (own your job) and are still
trading time for money; as a "Business Owner" you
are leveraging other people's time, energy and mind
to make money for you; and as an "Investor" your
money works for you. Reading books like these will
shift your mindset and perspective and will help you
gauge where you are and which model is best for you.
Gather a book list from business people you know
and read them, study them and implement what they
teach.

**Market Research**:  Start doing market research on the type of business you want to start.  Research the best of the best in your industry and learn about every aspect of their business model, find out what works and figure out how you can do it better or what you could do differently that will set you above the rest.  You may also want to research the "not so very best" of your industry and figure out what isn't working and make sure you DON'T do that!  If they're still in business, they are still serving their customer's needs in some way, so don't discount what you can learn from them entirely.  Find out who your competition is and visit their establishment (if you can) to get an "insider" view of how they run things.  Be curious and inquisitive with their staff.  Gather as much information as you can about your industry and potential competition.  Figure out the biggest problem your competition has and tailor your business around the solution only your business can provide.  Can you dial your business down to a specific niche and create a product or service that solves your ideal client's biggest problem? Your market research will answer this question.

**Financial Resources**: The biggest hurdle new business owners have is obtaining seed money or financial backing.  Most new business owners pool their own money, use credit cards and get personal loans from family members and friends. While this is a great way to fund your dream initially, there are other resources available if you have the right structures in place for your business.

There are plenty of small business loans and grants available. This is why having your personal finances in order is important for your business; it allows you to leverage your credit worthiness to fund your dream.

BUILDING THE "STRUCTURE" FOR YOUR BUSINESS

What I'm referring to is building the infrastructure of your business and not necessarily a literal structure. This means having all of the integral parts of your business in place such as your business plan, having your business name incorporated in your state, building out your website, setting up your merchant account (on and/or offline), setting up your social network profiles, creating your marketing materials and plan, leasing an office space or setting up your home office, etc.

You're probably thinking to yourself, "holy cow, that's a lot of work!", but remember, that's only coming from your current frame of mind, which may still be in the "Employee" mindset.

When you become a business owner, you'll learn about "Leverage" and "Outsourcing"; which means to pay others for their expertise for your benefit. Of course, there will be many things you will have to take on yourself, but for the most part, many of these things can be outsourced to a professional.

Once you have the ball rolling on these things, you'll be a few steps closer to opening your doors for business.

# 7

## Step 6: Determine What Kind of Lifestyle You Desire

**MY HUSBAND AND** I knew once we had kids we wanted to be the primary influences in their lives. We wanted to be able to make them breakfast every morning, see them off to school and be there when they got home to help them with their homework. We also wanted to be able to manage our own work schedule and spend quality time with our friends and family. We like to travel, so we incorporate family trips and have new experiences on a regular basis. When we first got together, we would dream out loud and list all of the things we wanted to experience together. We both came from humble beginnings and never got to experience many extravagancies or luxuries. So we treat ourselves to nice hotels and dinners when we travel, not because we are any better than anyone else, but because it reminds us of our journey and how far we've come. We created a lifestyle that is free of stress and worry and filled with lots of love and adventure. We also give back to the communities of the destinations we travel to by taking advantage of volunteering opportunities. We've been able to give our children experiences that nourish their spirit and give them a sense of belonging in the world. It's important to us that our children know the value of who they are and how they can contribute to the world around them. Everything we've been able to create has come from knowing what kind of life we wanted to live and lead. We strongly believe in living by example and our life-style is a reflection of who we are, what our values are, and where we spend our time.

Time is our most precious commodity; once it's spent, we'll never get it back, so we must spend it wisely. Take stock of where you're spending your time and if it's the highest use of it. Are you spending it on things that are important to you and on things that are in line with your core values?

The average American spends 5 hours a day in front of the television and while this is a nice way to wind down and disconnect after a hard day's work, we all have to ask ourselves if it's something that is con-tributing to the lifestyle we want to create. That's not to say everything on T.V. is bad, but is it elevating the quality of your life? What would it mean to you if you had an extra 30-35 hours a week to spend on things that were important to you? What would you do with your time? Would you spend it with your family and friends; take those dance lessons you've been dying to take; spend more time in nature; or teach your child how to ride a bike? How we spend our time is directly proportionate to the quality of our lives and we must align our values with where we spend our time.

LET YOURSELF DREAM!

Imagine you had a limitless supply of money and time. What would you do? Where would you go? Where would you stay? The Conrad Hilton, The Ritz Carlton or Four Seasons; or would you opt for a fancy boutique hotel or a quaint bed & breakfast?  Would you rent a nice luxury car or would you hire a driver? Would you hire a private jet, fly first class or opt to fly coach?

How would you share your wealth?  Would you start your own non-profit foundation or would you align yourself with a foundation that is near and dear to your heart? Or would you do both?

If you have children, get them involved! Imagine your child had a book report to do on Rome, what would it be like and feel like to take your child to Rome for a week and have them learn the history of the country IN the country versus reading about it from a book!

Get your imagination flowing and go BIG! If it feels uncomfortable, go even BIGGER!  Let yourself ponder the lifestyle you TRULY desire and write those experiences down.  Also write down your core values and how you can mold your experiences around what matters to you most.

## What Can You Do Now?

Start cultivating and creating experiences that are in alignment with the lifestyle you want. If giving back is important to you, what can you do now to make a contribution to your neighborhood or city? If you love to travel and can't yet afford a big trip, can you plan a short trip to a city you've never been to around your area? If you have children and want to spend more time with them, what kind of activities can you do together that will teach them a valuable life lesson? Take small steps in the direction of the lifestyle you want and make those experiences REAL for yourself by experiencing them, no matter how small it is.

When you do this, it creates new pathways in your brain that gets filed under "new lifestyle". If you can create enough experiences, you'll eventually believe that this lifestyle can be true for you and then you'll automatically create bigger and better experiences.

Remember, how you live and the quality of your life is a reflection of who you are and where you spend your time. Start small and keep upgrading. Live life differently and you'll have the lifestyle you ultimately desire.

# 8

## Step 7: Launch Your Business & Structure Your Business Around Your Lifestyle

**IT'S THE BIG** day: Grand Opening Day! You've got all the details in place and you're ready to open the doors to your business. You've got the keys to your office, your staff is lined up and ready to go and before you unlock the door, you hear the phone ring, which means your marketing paid off and your first customer is waiting to buy. You take a deep breath and enter into your new life. You feel waves of pride, accomplishment and gratitude rush through your body like an electrical current. You did it and boy, does it feel good!

All of your hard work has come to fruition. You're not just a business owner, you're a person who has taken ownership of your life and destiny. I can't tell you how awesome it feels to see someone step into his or her new reality; when the dream is no longer a dream. My husband and I experienced it and have seen many of our clients accomplish dreams they thought were not possible.

There are many business opportunities out there for you to jump into but we believe in building a business of your own. It becomes your baby and when it becomes a thriving business, you can look back and say, "I built this". It will become your living legacy and a vision of possibility for the people in your life. No one can take away the lessons you learned along the way or the person you became in the process.

As you can see, launching a business takes a lot of hard work. It requires you to look at yourself differently; to confront and push through fears that have held you back; and it requires you to do things you've never done before. Not everyone is willing to do the work that's required, but "if you're willing and obedient, you shall eat the good of the land", and that's the truth.

### Work/Life Balance

I encourage you to work smart when it comes to your business. Understand that you don't have to do it all yourself. The purpose of creating and launching your business is so that you can create a lifestyle that is balanced, peaceful and harmonious with the rest of your life. What good is a life you can't enjoy? I know plenty of people who don't have a life because they own their job. It doesn't have to be this way. You are in control of your time and where you spend it, so create a way to have it all.  Schedule your work around your lifestyle. You can be as strict or as flexible as you'd like with your work schedule, that's up to you, but schedule time for the things that matter to you too.  Make time for your family and friends; take time to read and continue your personal development; treat yourself to self-care on a regular basis; make time for exercise; and nourish your spirit as often as you can.  Make balance a priority.

You deserve the absolute best that life has to offer and I believe you can be, do and have anything you desire.  Wishing you the best on your journey to becoming the person you are meant to be. Remember It Starts With You!

## Gratitude

**THANK YOU FOR** taking the time to read this book, it means the world to me. I hope this has given you tremendous value and insight on your journey to becoming a thriving entrepreneur. God Bless!

## Special Bonus:

VISIT WWW.SHYRASMITH.COM TO learn how you can get a free 30 minute consultation with me. I am offering this as a special "Thank You" bonus for those who have purchased this book. This is a Limited Time Offer, so head on over and submit your information today!

## About the Author

**SHYRA SMITH** is a marketing guru, self-discovery expert, speaker and author who has been known to teach others to identify capabilities within themselves so that they can live the life they want to live. Sometimes you may know where you want to go or where you want to be but just get stuck in a limiting belief system, foster ineffective habits or have an inability to stay focused. Shyra is known for teaching step-by-step methods to better assist in achieving ones goals.

## One Last Thing...

**IF YOU ENJOYED** this book or found it useful I'd be very grateful if you'd post a short review on Amazon or email me at shyra@shyrasmith.com.Your support really does make a difference and I read all the reviews personally so I can get your feedback and make my books even better.

Thanks again for your support!